God Hears Her

A Joyful Christmas

31 Morning & Evening Devotions

Our Daily Bread
Publishing™

God Hears Her, A Joyful Christmas: 31 Morning and Evening Devotions
© 2021 by Our Daily Bread Publishing

Most of the devotional readings collected in this book were first published over a span of years in the *Our Daily Bread* devotional booklets that are distributed around the world in more than fifty languages.

Requests for permission to quote from this book should be directed to: Permissions Department, Our Daily Bread Publishing, PO Box 3566, Grand Rapids, MI 49501, or contact us by email at permissionsdept@odb.org.

Design: Jody Langley
Cover Illustration: Frimages/istockphoto
Interior Illustrations: Every Tuesday

ISBN: 978-1-64070-122-9

Printed in China

21 22 23 24 25 26 27 28 / 8 7 6 5 4 3 2 1

Introduction

Finances were tight, and Dot wanted to make next Christmas special for her three young boys. So early in January, she found three shiny bicycles at the local department store and put them on layaway. For the next eleven months, she scrimped—creatively saving money from her 75-cents-an-hour wage to make Christmas a joyful occasion for her boys.

But it wasn't enough.

A week before Christmas, she was still $14.50 short. Her son Ricky asked whether she had checked the piggy bank.

"I *know* there's not $14.50 worth of pennies in there," his mother told him.

To her amazement, when each coin was poured out, then carefully tallied, the amount equaled $15.50: enough to purchase the bikes and—with the extra dollar—to put gas in their car's tank to pick them up!

Many years later, Dot would call it God's *Christmas miracle* for their family. How like our humble God (Philippians 2:8) to use something simple and ordinary, like a piggy bank, to give pure joy.

More than two thousand years ago, God himself came to us in the most ordinary of ways, through the pain and struggle of childbirth. Upon entering our world, Jesus joined an ordinary family who experienced the challenges, joys, and beauty of everyday life. The outcome of His humble, commonplace—yet miraculous— entrance into the world? Pure joy (Luke 2:10).

Years later, Jesus hung from a wooden cross, dying. Suffering, He stayed faithful to His mission, drinking the cup His Father had given him until *it was finished* (John 18:11; 19:30). How was He able to complete His task and endure such pain? Scripture tells us it was because of joy (Hebrews 12:2). Christ's joy in His eternal purpose, in what lay ahead for Him—for all of us—enabled Him to finish His work so we could receive the world's greatest gift: a personal relationship with our Savior.

This Christmas, the women writers of *Our Daily Bread* invite you into this joy. For many, the "holiday season" is a time of both celebration and sorrow, laughter and loneliness. Whatever your highs and lows, spend time with Jesus at the beginning and close of your day, with these morning and evening devotions. Lovingly written by the diverse family at Our Daily Bread Ministries, each entry contains a Scripture passage to read and a devotional with an inspiring story to help you listen to the very heart of God.

As you soak in God's presence while reading *God Hears Her, A Joyful Christmas,* may you grow ever more confident of God's faithfulness to you. No matter the hardships you encounter, the scars you carry, the fears you face, you can rest assured: God is *for* you. Your Savior is quietly, humbly—yet miraculously—working on your behalf: Creating beauty out of ashes. Hope out of sadness. New beginnings out of loss. And, as He has since entering our world so long ago, offering you—and all of us—His overflowing, forever joy.

> I have told you these things so
> that you will be filled with my joy.
> Yes, your joy will overflow!
>
> (John 15:11 NLT)

—Anna Haggard
Associate Content Editor
Our Daily Bread Publishing

December 1

MORNING

I bring you good news
that will cause great
joy for all the people.

Luke 2:10

JOY

Luke 2:8–12

After Adam and Eve disobeyed God in the garden of Eden, joy was lost. God expelled them from Eden to prevent something worse from happening. If they had eaten from the tree of life after eating from the tree of knowledge of good and evil, they would have lived forever in their misery.

Life outside the garden was not easy. Adam and Eve had to work hard for their food. The reality of death was everywhere, and animals preyed on one another. Even worse, the couple's firstborn son murdered his younger brother. What could be worse? Sin had pierced their lives, and the couple could not stop joy from draining out.

But God had a plan to restore joy for mankind. Joy was lost in the garden when death came, but joy returned through birth—the birth of God's own Son at Bethlehem. "I bring you good news that will cause great joy for all the people" (Luke 2:10). Jesus grew up to heal the sick, give sight to the blind, and raise the dead. But this was just a taste of things to come. Jesus entered our world, experienced our sorrow, and conquered death—giving us hope that He will keep His promise to end pain, and eliminate sorrow and death (John 11:25–26; 1 Corinthians 15:3–4; Revelation 21:4).

No wonder Christmas is the season of joy!　　　　*—Julie*

Delight in the joy of the good news

December 1

EVENING

☆ ☆ ☆

Godliness with
contentment is
great gain.

1 Timothy 6:6

THE YARD-SALE CHRISTMAS

1 Timothy 6:6–10, 17–19

A mom felt she'd been overspending on family Christmas gifts, so one year she decided to try something different. For a few months before the holiday, she scrounged through yard sales for inexpensive, used items. She bought more than usual but for far less money. On Christmas Eve, her children excitedly opened gift after gift after gift. The next day there were more! Mom had felt guilty about not getting new gifts so she had additional gifts for Christmas morning. The kids began opening them but quickly complained, "We're too tired to open any more! You've given us so much!" That's not a typical response from children on a Christmas morning!

God has blessed us with so much, but it seems we're always looking for more: a bigger house, a better car, a larger bank account, or [fill in the blank]. Paul encouraged Timothy to remind people in his congregation that "we brought nothing into this world, and we can take nothing out of it. But if we have food and clothing, we will be content with that" (1 Timothy 6:7–8).

God has given us our very breath and life—besides providing for our needs. How refreshing it might be to enjoy and be content with His gifts and to say, *You've given us so much! We don't need more.* "Godliness with contentment is great gain" (v. 6).

—*Anne*

Be content with the abundance of unmerited joy our gracious Lord provides

December 2

MORNING

The Word became flesh and
made his dwelling among us.
We have seen his glory, the
glory of the one and only Son,
who came from the Father.

John 1:14

A CHRISTMAS LETTER

John 1:1–14

Every Christmas, a friend of mine writes a long letter to his wife, reviewing the events of the year and dreaming about the future. He always tells her how much he loves her, and why. He also writes a letter to each of his daughters. His words of love make an unforgettable Christmas present.

We could say that the original Christmas love letter was Jesus, the Word made flesh. John highlights this truth in his gospel: "In the beginning was the Word, and the Word was with God, and the Word was God" (John 1:1). In ancient philosophy, the Greek for Word, *logos*, suggested a divine mind or order that unites reality, but John expands the definition to reveal the Word as a person: Jesus, the Son of God who was "with God in the beginning" (v. 2). This Word, the Father's "one and only Son," "became flesh and made his dwelling among us" (v. 14). Through Jesus the Word, God reveals himself perfectly.

Theologians have grappled with this beautiful mystery for centuries. However much we may not understand, we can be certain that Jesus as the Word gives light to our dark world (v. 9). If we believe in Him, we can experience the gift of being God's beloved children (v. 12).

Jesus, God's love letter to us, has come and made His home among us. What an amazing Christmas gift! —*Amy*

Revel in the joy of being God's beloved child

December 2

EVENING

Ascribe to the Lᴏʀᴅ the
glory due his name;
bring an offering and
come into his courts.

Psalm 96:8

OUR PERFECT GIFT

Romans 12:1-8

Every year our local botanical garden hosts a celebration of Christmas around the world. My favorite display is a French nativity. Instead of the traditional scene showing shepherds and wise men with gifts of gold, frankincense, and myrrh gathered around the manger, it shows French villagers bringing their gifts to baby Jesus. They bring bread, wine, cheese, flowers, and other items that God has given them the ability to produce. This reminds me of the Old Testament command to bring the firstfruits of our labor to the house of the Lord (Exodus 23:16–19). This depiction of the nativity illustrates that everything we have comes from God, so the only thing we have to give is something that God has given us.

When Paul instructed the Romans to present themselves as a living sacrifice (12:1), he was telling them to give back to God what God had given them—their own selves. This includes the gifts He gave them, even their ability to earn a living. We know that God gives people special abilities. Some, like David, were skilled in music (1 Samuel 16:18). Some, like Bezalel and Oholiab, were skilled in artistic works (Exodus 35:30–35). Others have skill in writing, teaching, gardening, and many other things.

When we give back to God what He has first given to us, we give Him the perfect gift—ourselves. *—Julie*

Savor the joy of serving God with
your abilities

December 3

MORNING

My soul glorifies the Lord
and my spirit rejoices
in God my Savior.

Luke 1:46–47

A MOSAIC OF BEAUTY

Luke 1:46–55

Sitting in the courtyard of the Church of the Visitation in Ein Karem, Israel, I was overwhelmed with the beautiful display of sixty-seven mosaics containing the words of Luke 1:46–55 in as many languages. Traditionally known as the Magnificat from the Latin "to magnify," these verses are Mary's joyous response to the announcement that she will be the mother of the Messiah.

Each plaque contains Mary's words, including: "My soul glorifies the Lord and my spirit rejoices in God my Savior. . . . For the Mighty One has done great things for me" (vv. 46–49). The biblical hymn etched in the tiles is a song of praise as Mary recounts the faithfulness of God to her and the nation of Israel.

A grateful recipient of God's grace, Mary rejoices in her salvation (v. 47). She acknowledges that God's mercy has extended to the Israelites for generations (v. 50). Looking back over God's care for the Israelites, Mary praises God for His powerful acts on behalf of His people (v. 51). She also thanks God, recognizing that her daily provision comes from His hand (v. 53).

Mary shows us that recounting the great things God has done for us is a way to express praise and can lead us to rejoice. This Christmas season, consider God's goodness as you reflect on the year. In doing so, you may create a mosaic of great beauty with your words of praise. —*Lisa*

Reflect on the joy of praising Jesus

December 3

EVENING

✦ ✦ ✦

Weeping may stay for
the night, but rejoicing
comes in the morning.

Psalm 30:5

ALWAYS WINTER

Psalm 30:4-12

Unlike some of my family—the ones who can't wait to go downhill skiing—I don't look forward to winter. When the first snowflake falls, I immediately start calculating how many months of Michigan winter are left.

Imagine C. S. Lewis's fictional world of Narnia, where for a hundred years it was always winter. Cold, wet snow—with no hope of springtime ever arriving to wipe away the memories of icy temperatures and piles of white stuff. But worst of all, in Narnia, Christmas never came. Always winter and never Christmas! To me, the best part of winter is the anticipation, excitement, and wonder of Christmas. Life is bleak when you have nothing to look forward to.

There are some whose souls are locked in winter. The hardness of life has frozen their hearts. Disappointed with life, they find that each day is filled with despair. "Weeping may stay for the night," the psalmist tells us, "but rejoicing comes in the morning" (Psalm 30:5). In the darkest times of our lives, God longs to turn our "wailing into dancing" (v. 11).

David wrote, "When anxiety was great within me, your consolation brought me joy" (Psalm 94:19). If you cry out to God in the midst of your "winter," you can experience the joy of the Christ of Christmas today.   —*Cindy*

Contemplate the joy of anticipation

December 4

MORNING

The Word became flesh and
made his dwelling among
us. We have seen his glory,
the glory as of the one and
only Son, who came from the
Father, full of grace and truth.

John 1:14

THE TIME OF OUR REJOICING

Deuteronomy 31:9–13

When Christmas displays go up before Halloween displays come down, I long for the days when people didn't think about Christmas until after Thanksgiving. However, there may be a legitimate reason to celebrate Christmas in October.

No one knows the exact day when Jesus was born, but December 25 is unlikely. His birth may have been in autumn, when the weather was still warm enough for shepherds to be outdoors with their flocks. We know that Jesus was crucified on Passover, and that the Holy Spirit came on Pentecost. So some scholars have reasoned that Jesus's birth may have occurred on another Jewish holiday, the Feast of Tabernacles, or Sukkot.

Although we cannot know for sure, we do know that it would be in keeping with God's way of working to send His Son—the Word made flesh who "dwelt" ("tabernacled") among us (John 1:14)—on the Feast of Tabernacles. Sukkot was a time when observant Jews lived in temporary dwellings and listened to the Word of the Lord being read (Deuteronomy 31:10–13).

For Jews, Sukkot is "the time of our rejoicing." For all of us, our time of rejoicing is the birth of Christ, who brings the joy of salvation to all the world. —*Julie*

Bask in the joy of your salvation

December 4

EVENING

Thanks be to God for
his indescribable gift!

2 Corinthians 9:15

A REFRESHING CHANGE

2 Corinthians 8:1–9

Starting each October, catalogs begin to fill up my mailbox advertising clothes, appliances, shoes, candles, books, music—more than I could ever need or want for myself or for loved ones at Christmas.

But a particular catalog I received one November was a refreshing change. It was filled with ways people could give to orphans, the poor, the hungry, the sick, and the disabled through an international Christian ministry. The note in the front of the catalog read: "Share the light and love of Jesus Christ with people whose lives are filled with darkness and despair." What a relief to think about something other than buying one more thing for someone who already has so much!

The Macedonian church was an example of generosity (2 Corinthians 8:1–6). They gave themselves first to the Lord, then to those helping the needy in Jerusalem. Paul encouraged the Corinthians to follow their example and Christ's, who gave himself and "became poor, so that [we] through his poverty might become rich" (v. 9).

Do you want a refreshing change this Christmas? Consider new ways to give yourself to the Lord and to those in need. It's a meaningful way to thank God for "His indescribable gift" of salvation through His Son.

—*Anne*

Cherish the joy of giving of yourself

December 5

MORNING

The Word became
flesh and made his
dwelling among us.

John 1:14

THE MEANING OF CHRISTMAS

Luke 1:26-38

Each year it seems that Christ's birth is acknowledged less and less during the Christmas season. An editorial in a British newspaper stated, "Christ has been detached from Christmas, and the season is now apparently just a time for being kind and ensuring that no one is lonely."

We have a magnificent opportunity to spread the good news that Jesus is the reason for the season. Here are three perspectives on the true meaning of Christmas that we can share with others:

- Christmas is a birthday celebration, honoring Jesus. God's Son took on human flesh and "made his dwelling among us" (John 1:14).
- Jesus came for our sake. He was born to die on a cross for our sins, and He was resurrected to give us forgiveness and eternal life (1 Corinthians 15:3–4).
- We can urge people to respond to Jesus with faith, accepting His offer of salvation (John 1:12; 3:16).

This time of year is more than just a season to be kind. Christmas is about Jesus—the real reason for the season. So, let's take the opportunity to tell others the miraculous story of Jesus, God's Son. And let's pray that many, like the wise men who came to worship the promised Savior (Matthew 2:1–2), will seek Him and find Him this year. —*Joanie*

Celebrate the joy of seeking to know Jesus better

December 5

EVENING

✦ ✦ ✦

I thank my God every
time I remember you.

Philippians 1:3

A BLESSING BOWL

Romans 1:1–10

The familiar bing of an arriving email caught my attention while I wrote at my computer. Usually I try to resist the temptation to check every email, but the subject line was too enticing: "You are a blessing."

Eagerly, I opened it to discover a faraway friend telling me she was praying for my family. Each week, she displays one Christmas card photo in her kitchen table "Blessing Bowl" and prays for that family. She wrote, "I thank my God every time I remember you" (Philippians 1:3) and then highlighted our efforts to share God's love with others—our "partnership" in the gospel.

Through my friend's intentional gesture, the apostle Paul's words to the Philippians came trickling into my inbox, creating the same joy in my heart I suspect readers received from his first-century thank-you note. It seems Paul made it a habit to speak his gratitude to those who worked alongside him. A similar phrase opens many of his letters: "I thank my God through Jesus Christ for all of you, because your faith is being reported all over the world" (Romans 1:8).

In the first century, Paul blessed his collaborators with a thank-you note of prayerfulness. In the twenty-first century, my friend used a Christmas photo and a Blessing Bowl to bring joy into my day. How might we thank those who serve in the mission of God with us today?　　　*—Elisa*

Appreciate the joy of the work of God's people

December 6

MORNING

You will fill me with
joy in your presence,
with eternal pleasures
at your right hand.

Psalm 16:11

PRESENTS OR PRESENCE?

1 John 2:24-29

Oswald Chambers once wrote: "It is not God's promises we need, it is [God] himself."

At Christmastime we often say, "God's presence is more important than presents." But the amount of time and effort we spend on shopping for gifts may indicate otherwise.

In certain parts of the world, people give gifts on December 6. By doing so, they have the rest of the month to focus on Jesus and the wonder of His birth, God's perfect gift to us.

When we say we want God's presence more than presents from others, perhaps we're being truthful. But how many of us can honestly say that we want God's presence more than His presents?

Often we want gifts from God more than we want God himself. We want health, wealth, knowledge, a better job, a better place to live. God may indeed want to give us these things, but we can't have them apart from Him. As David said, "You fill me with joy in your presence" (Psalm 16:11). Presents may make us happy for a time; earthly gifts from God may make us happy temporarily, but fullness of joy comes only when we remain in a right relationship with God.

So, what would Christmas be like if we truly celebrated God's presence?

—*Julie*

Rest in the joy of God's presence

December 6

EVENING

Blessed is the one who trusts in the LORD, whose confidence is in him.

Jeremiah 17:7

WE NEED HOPE

Colossians 1:3–14

Adam and Eve didn't need hope, because they didn't lack anything they needed. And they had every reason to think that life would go on as pleasantly as it started—with every good thing that God had given them to enjoy. But they put it all at risk for the one thing the serpent said that God had withheld: the knowledge of good and evil (Genesis 2:17; 3:5). So, when the serpent came with his offer, Eve was quick to indulge, and Adam was quick to follow (3:6). They got what they wanted: knowledge. But they lost what they had: innocence. With the loss of innocence came the need for hope—hope that their guilt and shame could be removed and goodness restored.

Christmas is the season of hope. Children hope for the latest popular toy or game. Families hope that everyone can make it home for the holidays. But the hope that Christmas commemorates is much bigger than our holiday desires. Jesus, the "Desire of All Nations" (Haggai 2:7 NKJV), has come! He has "rescued us from the dominion of darkness," bought our redemption, and forgiven our sins (Colossians 1:13–14). He even made it possible for us to be wise about what is good and innocent about what is evil (Romans 16:19). Christ in us gives us the hope of glory.

Praise God for the hope of Christmas!   —*Julie*

Lean into the joy and hope of Christmas

December 7

MORNING

When [Jesus] heard
that Lazarus was sick,
he stayed where he
was two more days.

John 11:6

DELAY MAY NOT MEAN DENIAL

John 11:21–35

My sons' birthdays are in December. When they were small, Angus quickly learned that if he didn't receive a longed-for toy for his birthday at the beginning of the month, it might be in his Christmas stocking. And if David didn't receive his gift for Christmas, it might appear for his birthday four days later. Delay didn't necessarily mean denial.

It was natural for Martha and Mary to send for Jesus when Lazarus became seriously ill (John 11:1–3). Perhaps they looked anxiously along the road for signs of His arrival, but Jesus didn't come. The funeral service had been over for four days when Jesus finally walked into town (v. 17).

Martha was blunt. "If you had been here," she said, "my brother would not have died" (v. 21). Then her faith flickered into certainty, "I know that even now God will give you whatever you ask" (v. 22). I wonder what she expected. Lazarus was dead, and she was wary about opening the tomb. And yet at a word from Jesus, Lazarus's spirit returned to his decaying body (vv. 41–44). Jesus had bypassed simply healing His sick friend in order to perform the far greater miracle of bringing him back to life.

Waiting for God's timing may give us a greater result than we had hoped for. —*Marion*

Remain steadfast in the joy of God's perfect timing

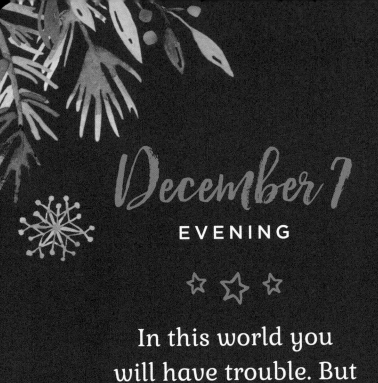

December 7

EVENING

In this world you
will have trouble. But
take heart! I have
overcome the world.

John 16:33

THE CHRIST OF CHRISTMAS

John 16:16–33

A discouraged Christian said to me one Christmas, "Christ's coming to earth has made little difference in my life. I still have so many trials." That made me think about the difference Jesus's life has made. I reflected on these four truths:

Jesus didn't remain a baby. He grew up "and became strong" (Luke 2:40) and had an effective ministry of teaching and healing (Matthew 9:35).

Our crucified Lord didn't remain in the grave. He arose to be our living Savior (Matthew 28:1–7; Revelation 1:18).

Our risen Savior didn't remain on the earth. He ascended to heaven to prepare a place for us and to send the Holy Spirit to indwell us (John 14:2, 25–26; Acts 1:9).

Our ascended Lord won't remain in heaven. He will come back to take us home to be with Him (John 14:3).

The birth of Christ has made a difference, but it doesn't mean we will have a trouble-free life. Jesus said, "In the world you will have trouble." But then He added, "Take heart, I have overcome the world" (John 16:33). Because Christ's presence and power is within us, we can triumph over trials. That's grounds for good cheer!

Instead of being overwhelmed by trials, we can face them confidently because Christ does make a difference.   —*Joanie*

Relax in the joy of Jesus's presence and power

December 8

MORNING

The virgin will conceive
and give birth to a
son, and they will call
him Immanuel.

Matthew 1:23

GOD WITH US

Matthew 1:18–23

"Christ with me, Christ before me, Christ behind me, Christ within me, Christ beneath me, Christ above me, Christ at my right, Christ at my left . . ." These hymn lyrics, written by the fifth-century Celtic Christian St. Patrick, echo in my mind when I read Matthew's account of Jesus's birth. They feel like a warm embrace, reminding me that I'm never alone.

Matthew's account tells us that God coming to dwell with His people is at the heart of Christmas. Quoting Isaiah's prophecy of a child who would be called Immanuel, which means "God with us" (Isaiah 7:14), Matthew points to the ultimate fulfillment of that prophecy—Jesus, the One born by the power of the Holy Spirit to be God with us. This truth is so central that Matthew begins and ends his gospel with it, concluding with Jesus's words to His disciples: "And surely I am with you always, to the very end of the age" (Matthew 28:20).

St. Patrick's lyrics remind me that Christ is with believers always through His Spirit living within. When I'm nervous or afraid, I can hold fast to His promises that He will never leave me. When I can't fall asleep, I can ask Him to give me His peace. When I'm celebrating and filled with joy, I can thank Him for His gracious work in my life.

Jesus, Immanuel—God with us. —*Amy*

Renew your joy through recognizing the Spirit's indwelling

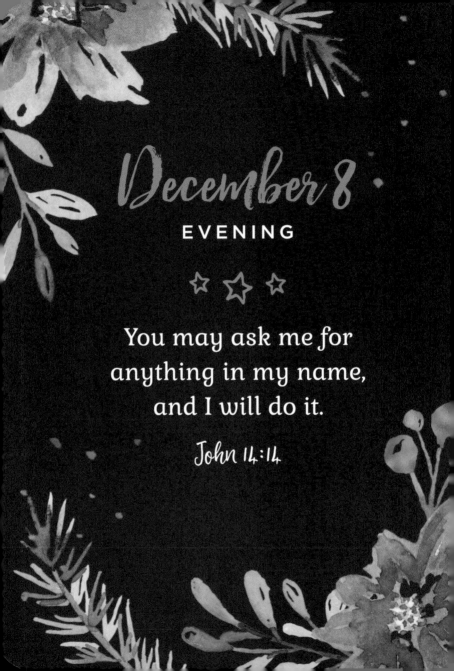

December 8

EVENING

✩ ✩ ✩

You may ask me for
anything in my name,
and I will do it.

John 14:14

PRAYING SHEEP

James 1:1–8

Two children who were dressed as sheep in the Christmas play at Kaw Prairie Community Church in De Soto, Missouri, had a special part. Whenever Murphy, the main character in the play, encountered a problem, the sheep (Maria and Luke) came on stage to offer a reminder of what he needed to do. One carried the sign: Just. The other carried the sign: Pray.

We've all been faced with situations when we didn't know what to do, or there was nothing we could do. When we're distressed, we probably don't want to hear someone flippantly say, "Just pray!" That answer seems too simplistic and can even feel hurtful if it's said unthinkingly.

But the simple answer "Just pray" is exactly what we need to do. During the days of the early church, James wrote to believers who were going through trials—difficulties that most of us know nothing about: stonings, imprisonment, and beatings for their faith. He told them to ask God for the wisdom and comfort to withstand those trials: "You should ask God, who gives generously to all without finding fault, and it will be given to you" (1:5).

When you encounter a problem, remember the simple instructions of the "Just Pray" sheep and talk to God about it. He'll give you what you need.

—Anne

Rekindle the joy of your salvation
through prayer

December 9

MORNING

Blessed are all who
wait for [the LORD].

Isaiah 30:18

WAITING . . .

Luke 2:22–38

For a few weeks in late autumn here in Michigan, it's hunting season. For a few weeks every year, licensed hunters are allowed to go out into the woods and hunt for various species of wildlife. Some hunters build elaborate tree stands high above the ground where they sit quietly for hours waiting for a deer to wander within range.

When I think of hunters who are so patient when it comes to waiting for deer, I think of how impatient we can be when we have to wait for God. We often equate "wait" with "waste." If we're waiting for something (or someone), we think we are doing nothing, which, in an accomplishment-crazed culture, seems like a waste of time.

But waiting serves many purposes. In particular, it proves our faith. Those whose faith is weak are often the first to give up waiting, while those with the strongest faith are willing to wait indefinitely.

When we read the Christmas story in Luke 2, we learn of two people who proved their faith by their willingness to wait. Simeon and Anna waited long, but their time wasn't wasted; it put them in a place where they could witness the coming of Messiah (vv. 22–38).

Not receiving an immediate answer to prayer is no reason to give up faith.

—*Julie*

Discover the joy of waiting for Jesus

December 9

EVENING

✩ ✩ ✩

Mary treasured up all
these things and pondered
them in her heart.

Luke 2:19

IF CHRISTMAS ISN'T MERCY

Luke 2:21–35

One Christmas I saw a cartoon that showed a boy gazing into a store window at a sign that read:

Have the Best Christmas Ever!

Thoughtfully, he said, "It's pretty hard to top the first one."

Years ago, my husband and I had an experience that drew our attention to that first Christmas. In mid-December, I gave birth prematurely to a much-wanted son. As our "Tiny Tim" struggled for life, he was rushed to another hospital. Then, miles away from us, he died all alone. Christmas that year was not jolly but grievous.

In our grief, however, God gave us a moving glimpse of His original Christmas. We saw that God also experienced empty arms, but in a much greater way. His baby Son had been born to die—a death that would bring eternal life to us all. Like Mary, we cherished and pondered these thoughts in our hearts. Slowly, the unhappiness that had threatened to diminish the meaning of Christmas enlarged it instead. In time, that Christmas became the most meaningful one we've ever had.

Once again, Christmas this year will be unavoidably sad for many people, perhaps for you. Take heart! Christmas needn't be merry to be meaningful. It's the Christ of Christmas we celebrate, not Christmas itself. Ponder Him!   —*Joanie*

Retain the joy of Jesus's advent, no matter what

December 10

MORNING

Thanks be to God for
his indescribable gift!

2 Corinthians 9:15

A GIVING COMPETITION

2 Corinthians 9:6–15

A television commercial I enjoy at Christmastime shows two neighbors in a friendly competition with each other to see who can spread the most Christmas cheer. Each keeps an eye on the other as he decorates his house and trees with lights. Then each upgrades his own property to look better than the other's. They start competing over who can give the most extravagantly to other neighbors, running around cheerfully sharing gifts.

In the real world, God's people aren't in a competition to see who can give the most. Instead, we are called to be "generous and willing to share" (1 Timothy 6:18). The apostle Paul instructed the church at Corinth: "Each of you should give what you have decided in your heart to give, not reluctantly or under compulsion, for God loves a cheerful giver" (2 Corinthians 9:7).

At Christmastime, as we share gifts with others, we remember the generosity of God toward us—He gave us His Son. Bible teacher Ray Stedman (1917–1992) said, "Jesus set aside His riches and entered into His creation in a state of poverty in order to enrich us all by His grace."

No gift-giving could ever compete with the Lord's extravagance. Thank God for the indescribable gift of Jesus! (v. 15).

—*Anne*

Remember the joy of God's great gift as you give and receive

December 10

EVENING

Bethlehem . . . out of you
will come for me one who
will be ruler over Israel.

Micah 5:2

"HOW MUCH LONGER?"

Micah 5:2-4

Iow much longer until it's Christmas?" When my children were little, they asked this question repeatedly. Although we used a daily Advent calendar to count down the days to Christmas, they still found the waiting excruciating.

We can easily recognize a child's struggle with waiting, but we might underestimate the challenge it can involve for all of God's people. Consider, for instance, those who received the message of the prophet Micah, who promised that out of Bethlehem would come a "ruler over Israel" (5:2) who would "stand and shepherd his flock in the strength of the Lord" (v. 4). The initial fulfillment of this prophecy came when Jesus was born in Bethlehem (Matthew 2:1) —after the people had waited some seven hundred years. But some of the prophecy's fulfillment is yet to come. For we wait in hope for the return of Jesus, when all of God's people will "live securely" and "his greatness will reach to the ends of the earth" (Micah 5:4). Then we will rejoice greatly, for our long wait will be over.

Most of us don't find waiting easy, but we can trust that God will honor His promises to be with us as we wait (Matthew 28:20). For when Jesus was born in little Bethlehem, He ushered in life in all its fullness (see John 10:10)—life without condemnation. We enjoy His presence with us today while we eagerly wait for His return.   —*Amy*

Wait with joy and peace on the future glory Jesus promises

December 11

MORNING

Trust in the LORD with
all your heart, and
lean not on your own
understanding.

Proverbs 3:5

THE FORGOTTEN MAN

Matthew 1:18–25

Amid all the Christmas activities, one man is often forgotten.

No, I don't mean the person whose birthday we're celebrating. Although we often fail to give Jesus first place as He deserves, we don't usually forget Him. I'm talking about Joseph—the man God trusted so much that He placed His Son in his home to love and nurture. What a responsibility!

Joseph truly is the forgotten man in the Christmas story. Yet his task was an important component of God's incredible plan. As we read the story of the birth of Jesus, we find that Joseph was just, righteous, merciful, protective, and courageous. But most of all, he was obedient. When the angel told him to take Mary as his wife, he obeyed (Matthew 1:24). And when the angel told him to flee to Egypt with Mary and Jesus, he did (2:13–14).

Just as Mary was carefully chosen to bear the Son of God, Joseph was deliberately chosen to provide for his young wife and the Christ-child. And trusting God, Joseph followed through on everything God asked him to do.

What is God asking of you today? Are you willing to commit yourself to do whatever He wants you to do?

We can learn much about obedience from Joseph, the forgotten man of Christmas.

—*Cindy*

Choose the joy that comes with obedience

December 11

EVENING

✦ ✦ ✦

Give, and it will be
given to you.

Luke 6:38

HOW TO REFLECT CHRIST

Luke 6:32-38

At a gas station one day, Staci encountered a woman who had left home without her bank card. Stranded with her baby, she was asking passersby for help. Although unemployed at the time, Staci spent $15 to put gas in the stranger's tank. Days later, Staci came home to find a gift basket of children's toys and other presents waiting on her porch. Friends of the stranger had reciprocated Staci's kindness and converted her $15 blessing into a memorable Christmas for her family.

This heartwarming story illustrates the point Jesus made when He said, "Give, and it will be given to you. A good measure, pressed down, shaken together and running over, will be poured into your lap. For with the measure you use, it will be measured to you" (Luke 6:38).

It can be tempting to hear this and focus on what we get out of giving, but doing so would miss the point. Jesus preceded that statement with this one: "Love your enemies, do good to them, and lend to them without expecting to get anything back. Then your reward will be great, and you will be children of the Most High, because he is kind to the ungrateful and wicked" (v. 35).

We don't give to get things; we give because God delights in our generosity. Our love for others reflects His loving heart toward us.

—Remi

Treasure the joy of giving in the
name of Jesus

December 12

MORNING

The Lord is not slow in
keeping his promise. . . .
Instead, he is patient with
you, not wanting anyone
to perish, but everyone
to come to repentance.

2 Peter 3:9

GOD WAITING

John 14:1-6

During the Christmas season we wait. We wait in traffic. We wait in checkout lines to purchase gifts. We wait for family to arrive. We wait to gather around a table filled with our favorite foods. We wait to open presents lovingly chosen.

All of this waiting can be a reminder to Christians that Christmas is a celebration of waiting for something much more important than holiday traditions. Like the ancient Israelites, we too are waiting for Jesus. Although He already came as the long-awaited Messiah, He has not yet come as ruler over all the earth. So today we wait for Christ's second coming.

Christmas reminds us that God also waits. He waits for people to see His glory, to admit that they are lost without Him, to say yes to His love, to receive His forgiveness, to turn away from sin. While we wait for His second coming, He waits for repentance. What seems to us like God's slowness in coming is instead His patience in waiting (2 Peter 3:9).

The Lord is waiting to have a relationship with those He loves. He made the first move when He came as baby Jesus and grew up to be the sacrificial Lamb. Now He waits for us to welcome Him into our lives as Savior and Lord.   —*Julie*

Experience the joy of repentance

December 12

EVENING

✫ ✫ ✫

And I will do whatever
you ask in my name, so
that the Father may be
glorified in the Son.

John 14:13

STAGECOACH PRAYER

John 15:7–14

Five-year-old Randy wanted a toy stagecoach for Christmas. While shopping with Mom, he found just the one he wanted. It was about six inches long and had cool wheels and dark brown plastic horses pulling it. "Mommy, I want this one. Pleeeease!" he begged. As young children sometimes do, he threw a tantrum, insisting that he get that stagecoach for Christmas. Mom said, "We'll see," and took him home.

Randy was sure he'd get what he asked for. Christmas morning came, and he opened the package confidently. Sure enough, it was the stagecoach he had begged for. He was so pleased. But then his older brother said, "You really did a dumb thing to insist on getting that coach. Mom bought you a much bigger one, but when you begged for that little one, she exchanged it!" Suddenly the small stagecoach didn't seem so appealing.

Sometimes we're like that with God. We pray about a specific need and tell Him how He ought to answer. We beg and plead—and God may even give us exactly what we ask for. But He may have had something better in mind.

Phillips Brooks once said, "Pray the largest prayers. You cannot think a prayer so large that God, in answering it, will not wish you had made it larger."

—*Anne*

Receive the joy that prayer brings to God's people

December 13

MORNING

Blessed are those
whose help is the God
of Jacob, whose hope is
in the LORD their God.

Psalm 146:5

EVERLASTING HOPE

Psalm 146

The week before Christmas, two months after my mom died, holiday shopping and decorating sat at the bottom of my priority list. I resisted my husband's attempts to comfort me as I grieved the loss of our family's faith-filled matriarch. I sulked as our son, Xavier, stretched and stapled strands of Christmas lights onto the inside walls of our home. Without a word, he plugged in the cord before he and his dad left for work.

As the colorful bulbs blinked, God gently drew me out of my darkness. No matter how painful the circumstances, my hope remained secure in the light of God's truth, which always reveals His unchanging character.

Psalm 146 affirms what God reminded me about on that difficult morning: My endless "hope is in the Lord," my helper, my mighty and merciful God (v. 5). As Creator of all, He "remains faithful forever" (v. 6). He "upholds the cause of the oppressed," protecting us and providing for us (v. 7). "The Lord lifts up those who are bowed down" (v. 8). He "watches over" us, "sustains" us, and will always be King (vv. 9–10).

Sometimes, when Christmas rolls around, our days will overflow with joyful moments. Sometimes, we'll face loss, experience hurt, or feel alone. But at all times, God promises to be our light in the darkness, offering us tangible help and everlasting hope.

—*Xochitl*

Warm your heart in the joy of God's light

December 13

EVENING

The people living in darkness
have seen a great light;
on those living in the land
of the shadow of death
a light has dawned.

Matthew 4:16

CHRISTMAS LIGHTS

Matthew 5:13–16

In December each year, a neighborhood of thirteen families near where we live sets up a dazzling display of three hundred thousand Christmas lights. People drive for miles and wait in line for hours to see the flashing, colorful lights and hear the music that is programmed to go with it. The sound-and-light display is so elaborate that it requires a network of computers to keep everything synchronized.

When I think about these holiday lights, I am reminded of the Light that makes Christmas a holiday for many—a single Light so bright that it illuminates the whole world with truth, justice, and love. This Light—Jesus—is everything the world is longing and looking for (Isaiah 9:2, 6–7). And He has told His followers to display His light so others will see and glorify God (Matthew 5:16).

Imagine if Christians worked as hard at shining and synchronizing the light of God's love as the families of that neighborhood work when they illuminate their street with Christmas lights. Perhaps then the people still living in darkness would make an effort to see this great Light. When Christians work together to display God's love, the gospel will shine more brightly and attract more people to Jesus—the Light of the world.   —*Julie*

Display God's joy by reflecting the Light of the world to others

December 14

MORNING

The virgin will conceive
and give birth to a
son, and will call
him Immanuel.

Isaiah 7:14

HOPE IN HIM

Isaiah 53

As we drove home from a Christmas party one evening, my family and I approached a small country church nestled between glittering snowbanks. From a distance, I could see its holiday display. Strings of white lights formed the capital letters: H-O-P-E. The sight of that word shining in the darkness reminded me that Jesus is, and always has been, the hope of humankind.

Before Jesus was born, people hoped for the Messiah—the One who would shoulder their sin and intercede with God on their behalf (Isaiah 53:12). They expected the Messiah to arrive through a virgin who would bear a son in Bethlehem and would name Him Immanuel (7:14), which means "God with us." The night Jesus was born, their hope was fulfilled (Luke 2:1–14).

Although we're no longer waiting for Jesus in the form of an infant, He is still the source of our hope. We watch for His second coming (Matthew 24:30); we anticipate the heavenly home He is preparing for us (John 14:2); and we dream of living with Him in His celestial city (1 Thessalonians 4:16). As Christians, we can look forward to the future because the baby in the manger was, and still is, "Christ Jesus, our hope" (1 Timothy 1:1).   —*Jennifer*

Anticipate the promised joy of a heavenly
home with Jesus

December 14

EVENING

✧ ✧ ✧

Praise be to the Lord, the God of Israel, because he has come to his people and redeemed them.

Luke 1:68

CHRISTMAS AT MACPHERSON

Luke 1:68–75

About 230 families and individuals live at MacPherson Gardens, Block 72 in my neighborhood. Each person has his or her own life story. On the tenth floor resides an elderly woman whose children have grown up, gotten married, and moved out. She lives by herself now. Just a few doors away from her is a young couple with two kids—a boy and a girl. And a few floors below lives a young man serving in the army. He has been to church before; maybe he will visit again on Christmas Day. I met these people last Christmas when our church went caroling in the neighborhood to spread Christmas cheer.

Every Christmas—as on the first Christmas—there are many people who do not know that God has entered into our world as a baby whose name is Jesus (Luke 1:68; 2:21). Or they do not know the significance of that event—it is "good news that will cause great joy for all the people" (2:10). Yes, all the people! Regardless of our nationality, culture, gender, or financial status, Jesus came to die for us and offer us complete forgiveness so we can be reconciled with Him and enjoy His love, joy, peace, and hope. All people—from the woman next door to the colleagues we have lunch with—need to hear this wonderful news!

On the first Christmas, the angels were the bearers of this joyous news. Today, God desires to work through us to take the story to others.

—Poh Fang

Participate in the joy of sharing Jesus's love with those who haven't heard

December 15

MORNING

Praise the LORD, my
soul, and forget not
all his benefits.

Psalm 103:2

WHAT CAN I GIVE HIM?

Psalm 103:1–18

One year, those responsible for decorating their church for Christmas decided to use the theme of "Christmas lists." Instead of decorating with the usual shiny gold and silver ornaments, they gave each person a red or green tag. On one side they were to write down the gift they would like from Jesus, and on the other they were to list the gift they would give to the One whose birth they were celebrating.

If you were to do this, what gift would you ask for and what would you offer? The Bible gives us lots of ideas. God promises to supply all our needs, so we might ask for a new job, help with financial problems, physical healing for ourselves or others, or a restored relationship. We might be wondering what our spiritual gift is that equips us for God's service. Many of these are listed in Romans 12 and 1 Corinthians 12. Or we might long to show more of the fruit of the Holy Spirit: to be more loving, joyful, peaceful, forbearing, kind and good, faithful, gentle, and self-controlled (Galatians 5:22–23).

The most important gift we can ever receive is God's gift of His Son, our Savior, and with Him forgiveness, restoration, and the promise of spiritual life that begins now and lasts forever. And the most important gift we can ever give is to give Jesus our heart.　　　　　　　　　　　　　　　　　　　　　　　　*—Marion*

Reap the joyous rewards of surrender to
Jesus

December 15

EVENING

✦ ✦ ✦

When the set time
had fully come, God
sent his Son.

Galatians 4:4

ON TIME

Luke 2:25-38

I used to joke that I was going to write a book titled *On Time*. Those who know me smile because they know I am often late. I rationalize that my lateness is due to optimism, not to lack of trying. I optimistically cling to the faulty belief that "this time" I will be able to get more done in less time than ever before. But I can't, and I don't, so I end up having to apologize yet again for my failure to show up on time.

In contrast, God is always on time. We may think He's late, but He's not. Throughout Scripture we read about people becoming impatient with God's timing. The Israelites waited and waited for the promised Messiah. Some gave up hope. But Simeon and Anna did not. They were in the temple daily praying and waiting (Luke 2:25–26, 37). And their faith was rewarded. They got to see the infant Jesus when Mary and Joseph brought Him to be dedicated (vv. 27–32, 38).

When we become discouraged because God doesn't respond according to our timetable, Christmas reminds us that "when the set time had fully come, God sent his Son, . . . that we might receive adoption to sonship" (Galatians 4:4–5). God's timing is always perfect, and it is worth the wait. —*Julie*

Recognize that there is joy in trusting God's timetable

December 16

MORNING

Teach [these words of mine] to your children.

Deuteronomy 11:19

FAITH INVESTMENTS

Deuteronomy 11:18–20

On his twelfth Christmas, the boy eagerly awaited the opening of the gifts under the tree. He was yearning for a new bike, but his hopes were dashed—the last present he opened was a dictionary. On the first page, he read: "To Charles from Mother and Daddy, 1958. With love and high hopes for your best work in school."

In the next decade, Chuck did do well in school. He graduated from college and later, aviation training. He became a pilot working overseas, fulfilling his passion to help people in need and to share Jesus with them. Now, some sixty years after receiving this gift, he shared the well-worn dictionary with his grandchildren. It had become for him a symbol of his parents' loving investment in his future, and Chuck still treasures it. But he's even more grateful for the daily investment his parents made in building his faith by teaching him about God and the Scriptures.

The author of Deuteronomy 11 talks about the importance of taking every opportunity to share the words of Scripture with children: "Teach them to your children, talking about them when you sit at home and when you walk along the road, when you lie down and when you get up" (v. 19).

For Chuck, the eternal values planted when he was a boy bloomed into a lifetime of service for his Savior. With God's enablement, who knows how much your investment in someone's spiritual growth will yield. —*Cindy*

Invest in the joy of others by encouraging their faith

December 16

EVENING

☆ ☆ ☆

God so loved the world.

John 3:16

JOY TO THE WORLD

John 3:1-8, 13-16

Every Christmas we decorate our home with nativity scenes from around the world. We have a German nativity pyramid, a manger scene fashioned out of olive wood from Bethlehem, and a brightly colored Mexican folk version. Our family favorite is a whimsical entry from Africa. Instead of the more traditional sheep and camels, a hippopotamus gazes contently at the baby Jesus.

The unique cultural perspective brought to life in these nativity scenes warms my heart as I ponder each beautiful reminder that Jesus's birth was not just for one nation or culture. It's good news for the whole earth, a reason for people from every country and ethnicity to rejoice.

The little baby depicted in each of our nativity scenes revealed that truth of God's heart for the entire world. As John wrote in relation to Christ's conversation with an inquisitive Pharisee named Nicodemus, "For God so loved the world that he gave his one and only Son, that whoever believes in him shall not perish but have eternal life" (John 3:16).

The gift of Jesus is good news for everyone. No matter where on earth you call home, Jesus's birth is God's offer of love and peace to you. And all who find new life in Christ, "from every tribe and language and people and nation" will one day celebrate God's glory forever and ever (Revelation 5:9).   —*Lisa*

Sing in your heart about Jesus's gift of joy to the world.

December 17

MORNING

Because your love is better than life, my lips will glorify you.

Psalm 63:3

NO GLITZ, NO GLORY

Isaiah 53:1–9

Looking at the handmade Christmas ornaments my son, Xavier, crafted over the years and the annual mismatched baubles Grandma had sent him, I couldn't figure out why I was not content with our decorations. I had always valued the creativity and memories each ornament represented. So, why did the allure of the retail stores' holiday displays tempt me to desire a tree adorned with perfectly matched bulbs, shimmering orbs, and satin ribbons?

As I began to turn away from our humble decor, I glimpsed a red, heart-shaped ornament with a simple phrase scripted on it—"Jesus, My Savior." How could I have forgotten that my family and my hope in Christ are the reasons I love celebrating Christmas? Our simple tree looked nothing like the trees in the storefronts, but the love behind every decoration made it beautiful.

Like our modest tree, the Messiah didn't meet the world's expectations in any way (Isaiah 53:2). Jesus "was despised and rejected" (v. 3). Yet, in an amazing display of love, He still chose to be "pierced for our transgressions" (v. 5). He endured punishment so we could enjoy peace (v. 5). Nothing is more beautiful than that.

With renewed gratitude for our imperfect decorations and our perfect Savior, I stopped longing for glitz and praised God for His glorious love. Sparkling adornments could never match the beauty of His sacrificial gift—Jesus.   —*Xochitl*

Notice that the joy of Jesus is without equal

December 17

EVENING

✩ ✩ ✩

Isn't this the carpenter's son? Isn't his mother's name Mary?

Matthew 13:55

EXPECT THE MESSIAH

Matthew 13:53-58

The repairman looked young—too young to fix our problem, a car that wouldn't start. "He's just a kid," my husband, Dan, whispered to me, showing his doubt. His disbelief in the young man sounded like the grumbling in Nazareth where citizens doubted who Jesus was.

"Isn't this the carpenter's son?" they asked (Matthew 13:55) when Jesus taught in the synagogue. Scoffing, they were surprised to hear that someone they knew was healing and teaching, and they asked, "Where did this man get this wisdom and these miraculous powers?" (v. 54). Instead of trusting in Jesus, they were offended by the authority He displayed (vv. 15, 58).

In this same way, we may struggle to trust in our Savior's wisdom and power, especially in the familiar and ordinary details of our daily lives. Failing to expect His help, we may miss out on the wonder of His life as it transforms our own (v. 58).

As Dan found, the help he needed stood right in front of him. Finally agreeing to accept the young man's aid, my husband allowed him to look at our old car's battery. By switching just one bolt, the mechanic had the car running in seconds— engine humming and lights ablaze. "It lit up like Christmas," Dan said.

So too may we expect and experience the Messiah bringing fresh light, life, and help into our daily journey with Him.

—Patricia

Journey with joy as Jesus daily supplies hope and light to your life

December 18

MORNING

For by one sacrifice
he has made perfect
forever those who are
being made holy.

Hebrews 10:14

HOW TO BE PERFECT

Romans 3:20-26

Christmas is the time of year when the pressure to be perfect intensifies. We imagine the perfect celebration and then put forth our best effort to make it happen. We shop for the perfect gifts. We plan the perfect Christmas Day meal. We choose the perfect greeting cards or write the perfect family letter. But our striving leads to discouragement and disappointment when our ability to imagine perfection exceeds our ability to implement it. The carefully chosen gift receives only a halfhearted thank you. Part of the meal is overcooked. We find a typo in our Christmas greeting after we've mailed the cards. Children fight over toys. Adults resurrect old arguments.

Instead of being discouraged, however, we can use our disappointment to remind ourselves of the reason Christmas is so important. We need Christmas because none of us is or can be all that we want to be—not for a month, a week, or even a day.

How much more meaningful our celebrations of Christ's birth would be if we would give up our faulty concept of perfection and focus instead on the perfection of our Savior, in whom we are made righteous (Romans 3:22).

If your Christmas celebration this year seems less than ideal, relax and let it be a reminder that the only way to be "made perfect forever" (Hebrews 10:14) is to live by faith in the righteousness of Christ.
—Julie

Let the joy of Jesus in your heart be your ultimate Christmas ideal

December 18

EVENING

I am reminded of your sincere faith, which first lived in your grandmother Lois and in your mother Eunice.

2 Timothy 1:5

A GOOD INHERITANCE

2 Timothy 1:1–5

Grandpa and Grandma Harris didn't have a lot of money, yet they managed to make each Christmas memorable for my cousins and me. There was always plenty of food, fun, and love. And from an early age we learned that it was Christ who made this celebration possible.

We want to leave the same legacy to our children. When we got together one recent December to share Christmas with family, we realized this wonderful tradition had started with Grandpa and Grandma. They couldn't leave us a monetary inheritance, but they were careful to plant the seeds of love, respect, and faith so that we—their children's children—might imitate their example.

In the Bible we read about grandma Lois and mom Eunice, who shared with Timothy the reality of genuine faith (2 Timothy 1:5). Their influence prepared this man to share the good news with many others.

We can prepare a spiritual inheritance for those whose lives we influence by living in close communion with God. In practical ways, we make His love a reality to others when we give them our undivided attention, show interest in what they think and do, and share life with them. We might even invite them to share in our celebrations! When our lives reflect the reality of God's love, we leave a lasting legacy for others.   —*Keila*

Make the joy of Jesus known to others as the best possible influence

December 19

MORNING

Christ came as high priest
of the good things that
are now already here.

Hebrews 9:11

JUST THE RIGHT TIME

Hebrews 9:11–22

The conductor stood on the podium, his eyes scanning the choir and orchestra. The singers arranged the music in their folders, found a comfortable position for standing, and held the folder where they could see the conductor just over the top. Orchestra members positioned their music on the stand, found a comfortable position in their seats, and then sat still. The conductor waited and watched until everyone was ready. Then, with a downbeat of his baton, the sounds of Handel's "Overture to Messiah" filled the cathedral.

With the sound swirling around me, I felt I was immersed in Christmas—when God, at just the right moment, signaled the downbeat and set in motion an overture that started with the birth of the Messiah, the "high priest of the good things that are now already here" (Hebrews 9:11).

Every Christmas, as we celebrate Christ's first coming with glorious music, I'm reminded that God's people, like choir and orchestra members, are getting ready for the next downbeat of the conductor when Christ will come again. On that day, we will participate with Him in the final movement of God's symphony of redemption—making all things new (Revelation 21:5). In anticipation, we need to keep our eyes on the conductor and make sure we are ready.   —*Julie*

Look ahead to the joy of all things being
made new

December 19

EVENING

✩ ✩ ✩

The child's father and
mother marveled at what
was said about him.

Luke 2:33

CANCELED CHRISTMAS

Luke 2:36-38

One year, we felt as if our Christmas was being canceled. Our flight to see family in Missouri was called off due to snow. It's been our tradition for quite a few years to celebrate Christmas with them, so we were greatly disappointed when we only got as far as Minnesota and had to return home to Michigan.

On Sunday, in a message we would have missed, our pastor spoke about expectations for Christmas. He caught my attention when he said, "If our expectations for Christmas are gifts and time with family, we have set our expectations too low. Those are enjoyable and things we're thankful for, but Christmas is the celebration of the coming of Christ and His redemption."

Simeon and Anna celebrated the coming of Jesus and His salvation when Joseph and Mary brought Him to the temple as a baby (Luke 2:25–38). Simeon, a man who was told by the Spirit that he would not die before he saw the Messiah, declared: "My eyes have seen your salvation" (v. 30). When Anna, a widow who served God, saw Jesus, she "spoke about the child to all who were looking forward to the redemption of Jerusalem" (v. 38).

We may experience disappointments or heartache during the Christmas season, but Jesus and His salvation always give us reason to celebrate.   —*Anne*

Praise God for the joy you can celebrate
because of Jesus's birth

December 20

MORNING

Today in the town of
David a Savior has been
born to you; he is the
Messiah, the Lord.

Luke 2:11

THE GIVER'S DELIGHT

Luke 2:4-14

Remember Tickle Me Elmo? Cabbage Patch Kids? The Furby? What do they have in common? Each rank among the twenty most popular Christmas gifts of all time. Also included on the list are familiar favorites such as Monopoly, the Nintendo Game Boy, and Wii.

We all delight in giving gifts at Christmas, but that's nothing compared to God's delight in giving the first Christmas gift. This gift came in the form of a baby, born in a Bethlehem manger (Luke 2:7).

Despite His humble birth, the Child's arrival was proclaimed by an angel who declared, "I bring you good news that will cause great joy for all the people. Today in the town of David a Savior has been born to you; he is the Messiah, the Lord" (vv. 10–11). Following this magnificent news, a "heavenly host" appeared, "praising God and saying, 'Glory to God in the highest heaven, and on earth peace to those on whom his favor rests'" (vv. 13–14).

This Christmas, enjoy giving gifts to your loved ones, but never lose sight of the reason for the giving—the spectacular favor of God on His creation crystallized in the gift of His own Son to save us from our sin. We give because He gave. May we worship Him in gratitude!

—*Remi*

Worship with joy and gratitude the One who gave us the ultimate Gift—Jesus

December 20

EVENING

⭐ ⭐ ⭐

Glory to God in
the highest.

Luke 2:14

NOW IS THE TIME

Luke 2:8-20

During our church's Christmas celebration, I watched the choir members assemble in front of the congregation while the music director rifled through papers on a slim black stand. The instruments began, and the singers launched into a well-known song that started with these words: "Come, now is the time to worship."

Although I expected to hear a time-honored Christmas carol, I smiled at the appropriate choice of music. Earlier that week I had been reading Luke's account of Jesus's birth, and I noticed that the first Christmas lacked our modern-day parties, gifts, and feasting—but it did include worship.

After the angel announced Jesus's birth to some wide-eyed shepherds, a chorus of angels began "praising God and saying: 'Glory to God in the highest.'" (Luke 2:13–14). The shepherds responded by running to Bethlehem where they found the newborn King lying in a barnyard bassinet. They returned to their fields "glorifying and praising God for all the things they had heard and seen" (v. 20). Coming face to face with the Son inspired the shepherds to worship the Father.

Today, consider your response to Jesus's arrival on earth. Is there room for worship in your heart on this day that celebrates His birth?

—*Jennifer*

Make room in your heart for the joy Jesus brings as you worship Him

December 21

MORNING

A star will come out of
Jacob; a scepter will
rise out of Israel.

Numbers 24:17

WISHING ON STARS

Matthew 2:1-10

On the night Jesus was born, the bright light of a single star announced His birth. It was an announcement that many had hoped and prayed for, yet many missed.

Perhaps they were like me. Perhaps their hopes were more like dreams and their prayers were more like wishes. Maybe they were looking for a star that would grant every whim, not a light that would reveal their sin.

Every Christmas when I sing in our church's annual Festival of Lights program, I wish for several things. I wish for those few magic moments when the choir is so perfectly in tune that I can't hear anyone, yet I can hear everyone. I think that's what the music of heaven will be like.

Every night when people are laughing at the drama, I wish that I could see what's so funny. But I always get stuck in a part of the choir loft that's behind the set.

Yes, I wish for these things, but I know that instead of wishing to hear the pure strains of a few songs, I ought to pray that I will hear God when He speaks.

Instead of wishing I could see the drama, I should pray that my eyes would see Jesus and not be distracted by the world.

Wishing is hoping I'll get what I want from God. A prayer is a plea that God will get what He wants from me. *—Julie*

Seek God's face to find the joy of following His heart

December 21

EVENING

His compassions never fail.
They are new every morning;
great is your faithfulness.

Lamentations 3:22–23

THE "HOPE FOR A BABY" TREE

Lamentations 3:1–3, 13–24

After wrapping the tree with clear twinkle lights, I tied pink and blue bows on its branches and christened it our "Hope for a Baby" Christmas tree. My husband and I had been waiting for a baby through adoption for more than four years. Surely by Christmas!

Every morning I stopped at the tree and prayed, reminding myself of God's faithfulness. On December 21 we received the news: no baby by Christmas. Devastated, I paused by the tree that had become a symbol of God's provision. Was God still faithful? Was I doing something wrong?

At times, God's apparent withholding results from His loving discipline. And other times God lovingly delays to renew our trust. In Lamentations, the prophet Jeremiah describes God's correction of Israel. The pain is palpable: "He pierced my heart with arrows from his quiver" (3:13). Through it all, Jeremiah also expresses ultimate trust in God's faithfulness: "his compassions never fail. They are new every morning; great is your faithfulness" (vv. 22–23).

I left the tree standing well beyond Christmas and continued my morning prayer. At last, on Easter weekend, we received our baby girl. God is always faithful, though not necessarily on our timeline nor always according to our desires.

My children are now in their thirties, but each year I set up a miniature version of the tree, reminding myself and others to hope in God's faithfulness.　　　　　　　　　　　—*Elisa*

Remind yourself that true joy comes from trusting wholeheartedly in our faithful God

December 22

MORNING

From infancy you have
known the Holy Scriptures,
. . . able to make you wise
for salvation through
faith in Christ Jesus.

2 Timothy 3:15

THE "MOM BOX"

2 Timothy 3:14-17

Each Christmas I give both of my daughters a "Mom box." Each box contains items to encourage them to be the best mothers they can be. It might have craft books or special projects, devotional books or tapes geared toward young moms, first-aid kits, recipes for cooking with kids—and often something personal like bubble bath for a little pampering after a tough day of mothering! It's become a tradition that Rosemary and Tanya have looked forward to every year for the last decade.

Encouraging our children to be good parents can begin even earlier. The best way is to start equipping them with the Word of God while they are still young.

The apostle Paul wrote that "from childhood" Timothy had known "the Holy Scriptures" (2 Timothy 3:15). And 2 Timothy 1:5 mentions the "sincere faith" of Timothy's mother and grandmother. That faithful teaching and spiritual influence helped to enable Timothy to be a godly man.

The Bible is our richest resource to help us raise children who will know and love Jesus. Nothing is more essential than "the Holy Scriptures" to equip them for all of life's challenges.

What are you doing to make the next generation "wise for salvation through faith"? (3:15).   —*Cindy*

Preserve generational joy by making God's
Word a family priority

December 22

EVENING

⭐ ⭐ ⭐

The Mighty One has done
great things for me.

Luke 1:49

THE BLESSING TREE

Luke 1:46–55

I read about a young couple whose business had failed, and they had little money to spend at Christmas. They were going to have to move out of their house after the new year. But they didn't want their holiday season to be spoiled because of it. So they decided to throw a party. When the guests arrived, they saw a cedar tree decorated with one string of lights and small rolled-up pieces of paper tied to the limbs with ribbon.

"Welcome to our 'blessing tree'!" they said, beaming. "In spite of hard times, God has blessed us in so many ways that we decided to dedicate our tree to Him. Each piece of paper describes a blessing He has given us this year."

This couple has faced more trials since then, but they have chosen to stay focused on the Lord. They often remark that the Christmas with the "blessing tree" was one of their most beautiful, because they could testify as Mary did: "My spirit rejoices in God my Savior . . . the Mighty One has done great things for me" (Luke 1:47–49).

Whatever your difficulties, they needn't spoil Christmas, for nothing can spoil Christ! Stay focused on Jesus and seek ways to share His blessings with others—perhaps through your own "blessing tree."

—*Joanie*

Focus on the joy of Jesus in your life—
and then spread the joy around

December 23

MORNING

But Mary treasured
up all these things
and pondered them
in her heart.

Luke 2:19

HEAVENLY ENCOUNTERS

Luke 2:8–19

Twinkle, Twinkle, Little Star" is one of my favorite lullabies. My mother would sing it to me, as I do with my children now. The lyrics "How I wonder what you are," highlight the mystery, majesty, and hopefulness found in the lights that paint our night sky. In 1806, author Jane Taylor published the poem "The Star," which has since been adapted into the song we love today. While she may not have known the impact these lyrics would have on generations to come, she clearly cherished them in her heart.

Mary, the mother of Jesus, experienced heavenly encounters throughout her miraculous pregnancy and the humble birth of the Savior. One of those moments was the visitation from shepherds who listened to the heaven-sent angels' announcement before rushing to Bethlehem (Luke 2:8–18). Arriving full of awe and excitement, they worshiped the Savior in Mary's presence. Although she was aware she had given birth to the Son of God (Luke 1:30–33), it's likely she didn't fully comprehend what that meant. Instead, she held each moment, such as the shepherds praising, dearly (2:19).

As we prepare for Christmas, we may not understand everything God has aligned to bring us to this day. But we can cherish each moment in our hearts—the humbling ones, the perplexing ones, and the joy-filled ones too—knowing that the Creator of the stars is always with us.

God, this season, please help us remember that just as you had a plan for Mary, you have one for us too.   —**Bree**

Be content with the abundance of unmerited joy our gracious Lord provides

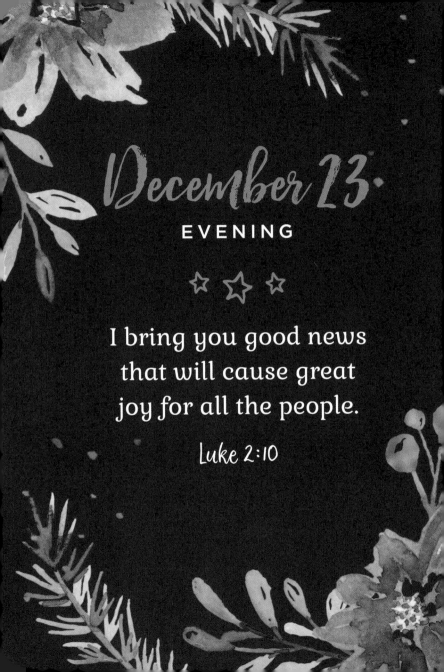

December 23·

EVENING

☆ ☆ ☆

I bring you good news
that will cause great
joy for all the people.

Luke 2:10

ONE SILENT NIGHT

Luke 2:1–14

Simon had emigrated from the Netherlands to the United States. His wife, Kay, and all three of their children had been born in the United States. Then Jenny married Roberto from Panama. Bill married Vania from Portugal. And Lucas married Bora from South Korea.

On Christmas Eve, as the family gathered for a celebration, they began singing "Silent Night" in their native tongues—a sweet sound indeed for the Lord of the earth to hear as they celebrated the birth of His Son.

Two thousand years ago, the silence of a quiet night ended abruptly when an angel told the shepherds a baby had been born: "I bring you good news that will cause great joy for all the people" (Luke 2:10). Then a multitude of angels began praising God, saying, "Glory to God in the highest heaven, and on earth peace to those on whom his favor rests." (v. 14). Christ the Lord, the Savior of the world, was born!

God's gracious gift, His Son, which was announced on that long-ago silent night, is still available to everyone—"every tribe and nation" (Titus 2:11–14; Revelation 5:9–10). "For God so loved the world that he gave his one and only Son, that whoever believes in him shall not perish but have eternal life" (John 3:16). —*Cindy*

Imagine the joy that would come to lost people worldwide if they knew about Jesus's love

December 24

MORNING

Sovereign Lord, . . . you
may now dismiss your
servant in peace.

Luke 2:29

A CHRISTMAS VISITOR

Luke 2:25–33

On Christmas Eve 1944, a man known as "Old Brinker" lay dying in a prison hospital, waiting for the makeshift Christmas service led by fellow prisoners. "When does the music start?" he asked William McDougall, who was imprisoned with him in Muntok Prison in Sumatra. "Soon," replied McDougall. "Good," replied the dying man. "Then I'll be able to compare them with the angels."

Although decades earlier Brinker had moved away from his faith in God, in his dying days he confessed his sins and found peace with Him. Instead of greeting others with a sour look, he would smile, which "was quite a transformation," said McDougall.

Brinker died peacefully after the choir of eleven emaciated prisoners sang his request, "Silent Night." Knowing that Brinker once again followed Jesus and would be united with God in heaven, McDougall observed, "Perhaps Death had been a welcome Christmas visitor to old Brinker."

How Brinker anticipated his death reminds me of Simeon, a holy man to whom the Holy Spirit revealed that "he would not die before he had seen the Lord's Messiah" (Luke 2:26). When Simeon saw Jesus in the temple, he exclaimed, "You may now dismiss your servant in peace. For my eyes have seen your salvation" (vv. 29–30).

As with Brinker, the greatest Christmas gift we can receive or share is that of saving faith in Jesus. —*Amy*

Think of the joy believers experience when our silent night comes and we actually see Jesus

December 24

EVENING

✦ ✦ ✦

All Scripture is
God-breathed.

2 Timothy 3:16

CURLING UP WITH A GOOD BOOK

2 Timothy 3:14–17

The small country of Iceland is a nation of readers. In fact, it's reported that each year this nation publishes and reads more books per person than any other country. On Christmas Eve, it's a tradition for Icelanders to give books to family and friends and then read long into the night. This tradition dates back to World War II, when imports were restricted but paper was cheap. Icelandic publishers began flooding the market with new titles in late fall. Now a catalog of the country's new releases is sent to every Icelandic home in mid-November. This tradition is known as the Christmas Book Flood.

We can be thankful God blessed so many with the ability to craft a good story and to educate, inspire, or motivate others through their words. There's nothing like a good book! The best-selling book of all, the Bible, was composed by many authors who wrote in poetry and prose—some great stories, some not so—but all of it inspired. As the apostle Paul reminded Timothy, "All Scripture is God-breathed and is useful for teaching, rebuking, correcting and training in righteousness" and equipping God's people "for every good work" (2 Timothy 3:16–17). Reading the Bible convicts, inspires, and helps us to live for Him—and guides us into the truth (2:15).

In our reading, let's not forget to find time to curl up with the greatest book of all, the Bible.　　　　　　　　　—*Alyson*

Explore the Bible to discover the many facets of the joy God provides His people

December 25

MORNING

Thanks be to God for
his indescribable gift!

2 Corinthians 9:15

A FRAGILE GIFT

Luke 2:1-7

When we give a fragile gift, we make sure it is marked on the box that contains it. The word FRAGILE is written with big letters because we don't want anyone to damage what is inside.

God's gift to us came in the most fragile package: a baby. Sometimes we imagine Christmas day as a beautiful scene on a postcard, but any mother can tell you it wasn't so. Mary was tired, probably insecure. It was her first child, and He was born in the most unsanitary conditions. She "wrapped Him in swaddling cloths, and laid Him in a manger, because there was no room for them in the inn" (Luke 2:7 NKJV).

A baby needs constant care. Babies cry, eat, sleep, and depend on their caregivers. They cannot make decisions. In Mary's day, infant mortality was high, and mothers often died in childbirth.

Why did God choose such a fragile way to send His Son to earth? Because Jesus had to be like us in order to save us. God's greatest gift came in the fragile body of a baby, but God took the risk because He loves us. Let us be thankful today for such a gift!

—*Keila*

Meditate on the reality that the joy of our salvation had its beginnings in a little baby boy

December 25

EVENING

☆ ☆ ☆

There was no guest room
available for them.

Luke 2:7

A GIFT OF SHELTER

Luke 2:1-7

Life was tough for Datha and her family. At age thirty-nine, she had a heart attack and bypass surgery and learned that she had coronary artery disease. A year later, her fifteen-year-old daughter Heather became paralyzed as the result of a car accident. Datha quit her job to take care of Heather, and the bills started piling up. Soon they would be facing eviction. Datha was so angry with God that she stopped praying.

Then came Christmas Eve. A young girl knocked on Datha's door. The girl wished her a "Merry Christmas," gave her an envelope, and left quickly. Inside was a gift that would cover Datha's housing needs for the next year. The attached note read, "Please accept this gift in honor of the Man whose birthday we celebrate on this holy night. Long ago, His family also had a shelter problem."

Luke 2 tells the story of Joseph and Mary as they searched for a shelter for Mary to deliver her baby. They found a place with the animals. Later in His life, Jesus said of himself, "The Son of Man has no place to lay his head" (Matthew 8:20).

Jesus understood Datha's troubles. He brought her hope and met her needs through others who contributed funds.

We can cast all our cares on Him (1 Peter 5:7). In Christ, we find shelter (Psalm 61:3–4).   *—Anne*

Grasp the joy of knowing that Jesus wants to carry our burdens and provide shelter for our hearts

December 26

MORNING

Mary treasured up all
these things and pondered
them in her heart.

Luke 2:19

A STRING OF YESES

Luke 2:15–19

One Christmas, my grandmother gave me a beautiful pearl necklace. The beautiful beads glowed about my neck until one day the string broke. Balls bounced in all directions off our home's hardwood flooring. Crawling over the planks, I recovered each tiny orb. On their own, they were small. But oh, when strung together, those pearls made such an impression!

Sometimes my yeses to God seem so insignificant—like those individual pearls. I compare myself to Mary, the mother of Jesus who was so fantastically obedient. She said yes when she embraced God's call for her to carry the Messiah. "'I am the Lord's servant,' Mary answered. 'May your word to me be fulfilled'" (Luke 1:38). Did she understand all that would be required of her? That an even bigger yes to relinquishing her Son on the cross loomed ahead?

After the visits of the angels and shepherds, Luke 2:19 tells us that Mary "treasured up all these things and pondered them in her heart." *Treasure* means to "store up." *Ponder* means to "thread together." The phrase is repeated of Mary in Luke 2:51. She would respond with many yeses over her lifetime.

As with Mary, the key to our obedience might be a threading together of various yeses to our Father's invitations, one at a time, until they string into the treasure of a surrendered life.

—*Elisa*

Say yes to the joy Jesus offers when we surrender our lives to Him.

December 26

EVENING

✩ ✩ ✩

Simeon took him
[Jesus] in his arms
and praised God.

Luke 2:28

NEWS WORTH SHARING

Luke 2:25–32

During the godless reign of the Spanish dictator Francisco Franco, a missionary climbed three flights of stairs, knocked on Isabela Gomez's apartment door, and handed her a Bible. Isabela read it and committed her life to Christ. Her newfound relationship with God made such a profound impact on her son Carlos that he sneaked into her bedroom one night, took the Bible from her bedside, and stayed up all night reading it. By dawn, he too had come face to face with Christ. He surrendered his life to Him and has spent the last thirty years telling others about Jesus.

Carlos met Christ in the pages of Scripture, but Simeon met Him in person. Simeon was a man of extraordinary faith. Moved by the Spirit, Luke 2:27 tells us, he went into the temple courts on the day Jesus was dedicated. There he encountered the Christ child, just as God had promised. Taking Jesus in his arms, Simeon praised God and testified to all who would listen, "My eyes have seen your salvation, . . . a light for revelation to the Gentiles and the glory of your people Israel" (Luke 2:30–32).

Simeon and Carlos demonstrate what happens when someone meets Jesus. Whether they encounter Him in person, like Simeon, or through reading the Scriptures, like Carlos, they can't keep Him to themselves. They must tell others about Him.

Who in your life needs to hear about Jesus? What hinders you from sharing Christ with them?

Father, help me be bold to tell others about Jesus. —*Lori*

Pray for courage and wisdom to share with others the unspeakable joy of knowing Jesus

December 27

MORNING

I am the resurrection
and the life. The one who
believes in me will live,
even though they die.

John 11:25

HAPPY CHRISTMAS!

John 3:13–18

One Easter morning when I walked into church I saw my friend and greeted her, "Happy Christmas!" I quickly corrected myself. "I mean, Happy Easter!"

"Can't have one without the other," she said with a smile.

How true! Without Christmas, there wouldn't be an Easter. And without the resurrection, Easter Sunday would be just another day. In fact, we wouldn't even be in church on that day.

Christmas and Easter are the most joyful celebrations of the year for the Christian. In the first, we celebrate the incarnation (God taking on flesh and coming into the world). "For God so loved the world that he gave his one and only Son" (John 3:16).

In the second, we celebrate Jesus's resurrection. "He is not here; he has risen!" the angel said (Luke 24:6). From the beginning of time, these two days were inextricably linked in the master plan of the Father. Jesus was born to die for our sins and to conquer death so we could live.

Which is more important? Christmas—the birth of the infant Jesus? Or Easter—the death and resurrection of the man, God's Son? Both are essential—and both are clear evidence of the Father's love for us.

Happy Christmas! And Happy Easter!   —*Cindy*

Balance the double blessing and joy of
both Jesus's birth and His death, burial,
and resurrection

December 27

EVENING

✦ ✦ ✦

[Mary] gave birth to
her firstborn, a son.
She wrapped him in
cloths and placed
him in a manger.

Luke 2:7

BECAUSE OF LOVE

Luke 2:1–7

In a recent year, I received some nice Christmas gifts—ski pants, a bracelet, and a Kindle reader. But what I enjoyed the most were the gifts of time with people: playing with nine grandnephews and grandnieces from out of state; having a niece and her husband and their young daughter attend our church's Christmas Eve service with us; visiting with a retired coworker and his wife who are suffering with some health issues; celebrating the season with longtime friends; reading the Christmas story with loved ones. These were all special gifts because of the love we share.

God the Father, because of love, sent a gift to this world two thousand years ago. Jesus was wrapped in cloths by His mother and placed in a manger (Luke 2:7). The shepherds knew He was an amazing gift because an angel announced His birth to them in the middle of the night while they were in their fields (vv. 8–14). They rushed to see Him and then couldn't help but share the news of this Gift with others (vv. 16–17). Yet many people later rejected Him, and He was crucified for our sins and buried in a borrowed tomb. But He rose from the tomb and now offers salvation to all who receive Him.

Thank you, God, for the Gift you gave—because of love.

—Anne

Recommit yourself to praising God for the joy of your salvation

December 28

MORNING

Once you were alienated
from God. . . . But now
he has reconciled you.

Colossians 1:21–22

PEACE

Colossians 1:19-29

In the days of Adam and Eve, peace was lost. As soon as they ate the forbidden fruit and realized their nakedness, they started blaming each other (Genesis 3:12–13) and introduced conflict to God's peaceful planet. Sadly, all of their descendants, including us, have followed their bad example. We blame others for our own bad choices and become angry when no one will accept the guilt. Blaming others for our unhappiness breaks apart families, churches, communities, and nations. We can't make peace because we're preoccupied with placing the blame.

Christmas is the season of peace. The Old Testament tells the story of how God set the stage to introduce the Prince of Peace (Isaiah 9:6). Jesus came to break the cycle of sin and blame by making peace for us with God "through his blood, shed on the cross" (Colossians 1:20). Instead of blaming us for all the trouble we cause, He bore the blame for all of us. He is now recruiting followers who, having received His forgiveness, want others to receive it as well.

When we accept forgiveness from God, we lose our desire to withhold it from others. And when we live in peace with God, we are eager to make peace with others. We can both give and receive the gift of peace this Christmas. —*Julie*

Give the gift of peace and joy to others

December 28

EVENING

✦ ✦ ✦

He will not shout or cry
out, or raise his voice
in the streets. A bruised
reed he will not break.

Isaiah 42:2–3

WINTER SNOW

Isaiah 42:1-4

In winter, I often wake to the beautiful surprise of a world blanketed in the peace and quiet of an early morning snow. Not loudly like a spring thunderstorm that announces its presence in the night, snow comes softly.

In "Winter Snow Song," Audrey Assad sings that Jesus could have come to earth in power like a hurricane, but instead He came quietly and slowly like the winter snow falling softly in the night outside my window.

Jesus's arrival took many by quiet surprise. Instead of being born in a palace, He was born in an unlikely place, a humble dwelling outside Bethlehem. And He slept in the only bed available, a manger (Luke 2:7). Instead of being attended by royalty and government officials, Jesus was welcomed by lowly shepherds (vv. 15–16). Instead of having wealth, Jesus's parents could only afford the inexpensive sacrifice of two birds when they presented Him at the temple (v. 24).

The unassuming way Jesus entered the world was foreshadowed by the prophet Isaiah, who prophesied the coming Savior would "not shout or cry out" (Isaiah 42:2) nor would He come in power that might break a damaged reed or extinguish a struggling flame (v. 3). Instead He came gently in order to draw us to himself with His offer of peace with God—a peace still available to anyone who believes the unexpected story of a Savior born in a manger.   —*Lisa*

Believe wholeheartedly in the One who offers peace and eternal security

December 29

MORNING

There will be no more
night. They will not need
the light of a lamp or the
light of the sun, for the Lord
God will give them light.

Revelation 22:5

DECEMBER DESIRE

Revelation 22:1-5

December is a month when people celebrate miracles. The Jewish tradition of Hanukkah—the Holiday of Lights—commemorates the time when a small amount of oil lasted eight days and kept the light in the temple from going out. And Christmas celebrates the coming of the "Light of the World," God in human form—Jesus.

A miracle is generally thought of as something that contradicts nature. But a true miracle is the introduction of God's supernatural power into our world in a way that suspends the laws of physics as we understand them.

In December, it seems that more of us are willing to suspend disbelief and entertain the possibility that "nature" is not the final authority. Even the nonreligious yearn for miracles. Deep down, everyone wants to believe that darkness, disease, and death can be overcome.

Perhaps the most wondrous thing about miracles is that it is God's nature to do the supernatural. The closing chapters of Scripture assure us that this "December desire" for all to be well will become a reality: "There shall be no more death or mourning or crying or pain" (Revelation 21:4). God will one day bring to an end the unnatural rule of Satan and begin His righteous reign as the rightful Ruler of the universe.   —*Julie*

Think about the joy of the end of Satan's rule
and the forever of Jesus's reign

December 29

EVENING

☆ ☆ ☆

Never will I leave you;
never will I forsake you.

Hebrews 13:5

ALL IS WELL

Recently, my husband and I were reacquainted with a young man we had known as a child many years ago. We fondly reminisced about a Christmas program when Matthew had sung—in a perfect boy soprano—the song "All Is Well" by Wayne Kirkpatrick and Michael W. Smith. It was a wonderful memory of a song beautifully sung.

The song reminds us to lift our voices in song as we recall that our Immanuel, our Savior was born. Look up the words and be edified by their reminder that God is with us.

To hear the words of that song at Christmastime is comforting to many. But some people are unable to absorb the message because their lives are in turmoil. They've experienced the loss of a loved one, persistent unemployment, a serious illness, or depression that will not go away. Their hearts loudly cry out, "All is not well—not for me!"

But for those of us who celebrate the birth of our Savior—despite the dark night of the soul we may experience—all is well because of Christ. We are not alone in our pain. God is beside us and promises never to leave (Hebrews 13:5). He promises that His grace will be sufficient (2 Corinthians 12:9). He promises to supply all our needs (Philippians 4:19). And He promises us the amazing gift of eternal life (John 10:27–28).

As we review God's promises, we can agree with the poet John Greenleaf Whittier, who wrote, "Before me, even as behind, God is, and all is well."

—Cindy

Review God's promises to remind yourself of the joy of knowing and obeying Him

December 30

MORNING

See what great love the
Father has lavished on
us, that we should be
called children of God!

1 John 3:1

TRULY AMAZING

Romans 5:6–11

I read these words on a young woman's personal website: "I just want to be loved—and he has to be amazing!"

Isn't that what we all want—to be loved, to feel cared for by someone? And so much the better if he or she is amazing!

The one who fits that description most fully is Jesus Christ. In a display of unprecedented love, He left His Father in heaven and came to earth as the baby we celebrate at Christmas (Luke 2). Then, after living a perfect life, He gave His life as an offering to God on the cross in our behalf (John 19:17–30). He took our place because we needed to be rescued from our sin and its death penalty. "While we were still sinners, Christ died for us" (Romans 5:8). Then three days later, the Father raised Jesus to life again (Matthew 28:1–8).

When we repent and receive Jesus's gift of amazing love, He becomes our Savior (John 1:12; Romans 5:9), Lord (John 13:14), Teacher (Matthew 23:8), and Friend (John 15:14). "See what great love the Father has lavished on us, that we should be called children of God!" (1 John 3:1).

Looking for someone to love you? Jesus loves us so much more than anyone else possibly could. And He is truly amazing!

—Anne

Accept Jesus's lavish love and bask in
the joy of His salvation

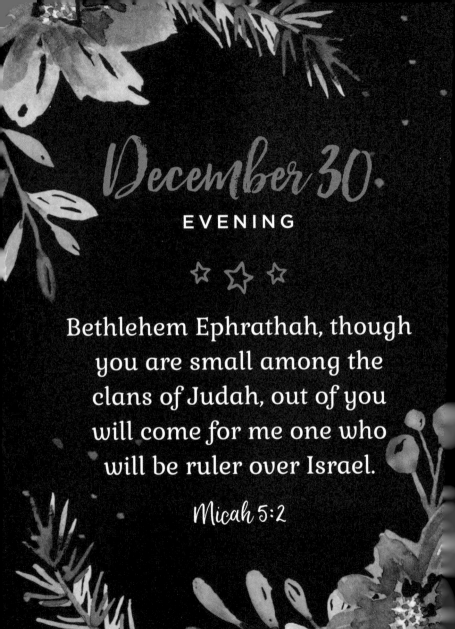

December 30

EVENING

✦ ✦ ✦

Bethlehem Ephrathah, though
you are small among the
clans of Judah, out of you
will come for me one who
will be ruler over Israel.

Micah 5:2

EAT THIS BREAD

Matthew 26:20-30

The Christmas season isn't the time of year when our thoughts naturally turn to the Last Supper—or what the Jews called Passover. But that particular Passover is critical to Christmas. After breaking bread and giving it to His disciples, Jesus said, "Take and eat; this is my body" (Matthew 26:26). Breaking bread was a traditional part of Passover, but adding "this is my body" was a striking departure from the familiar liturgy. The disciples must have been bewildered.

Later the meaning became clear. Jesus was born in Bethlehem, which means "house of Bread." He was laid in a manger—a feeding trough. He once said, "I am the living bread that came down from heaven. Whoever eats this bread will live forever. This bread is my flesh, which I will give for the life of the world" (John 6:51).

The prophet Micah indicated that One born in Bethlehem would rule over Israel (5:2). But not until Jesus came did anyone realize the uniqueness of this kingdom. Christ's rule would not be imposed upon anyone; it would be imparted to those who accepted this new citizenship.

As we sing of Bethlehem mangers, let's remember that the heaven-sent infant King came so that we might "eat this bread" and partake of His divine nature. *—Julie*

Marvel at God's eternal plan of salvation—
a plan that brings unspeakable joy

December 31

MORNING

[She] was a widow until
she was eighty-four. She
never left the temple but
worshiped night and day.

Luke 2:37

CHRISTIANS NEVER RETIRE

Luke 2:36–38

A few years ago, I sat across from Nell and her husband, Lairy, at a church dinner. Mrs. Nell was ninety-five years old and a founding member of our church. As she shared her recipe for orange salad, she paused, leaned over to her husband, and tapped the tablecloth.

"We can take these home and wash them," she said, referring to the linens. Then she turned back to me. "We can't do much these days, but we can do something."

In her younger days Nell had taught Sunday school, worked in Vacation Bible School, and sang in the choir. As she got older, she cooked our favorite dishes and washed church linens. Although her strength was declining as she aged, she kept serving God and His people. Mrs. Nell was a modern-day Anna.

Scholars believe the prophetess who greeted the baby Jesus in the temple was at least eighty-four years old. Widowed for most of her life, she worshiped God with "fasting and prayer night and day" (Luke 2:37). The Greek word Luke used to describe Anna's worship of God, *latreuō*, is translated "served" thirteen times elsewhere in the Bible. This alternate meaning beautifully describes how Anna worshiped—by serving.

While Anna and Mrs. Nell's labor of love may have gone unnoticed by most, God saw it. He rewarded Anna by allowing her to see the Christ child. I can only imagine how He'll reward Mrs. Nell. Both women inspire me to serve God faithfully all the days of my life.

What stage of life are you in right now? How can you worship God through your service?

Lord, help me worship You by serving You all the days of my life.

—*Lori*

Worship the Lord with joy by serving Him in the ways He provides

December 31

EVENING

Everyone whose heart
God had moved—
prepared to go up and
build the house of the
Lord in Jerusalem.

Ezra 1:5

BEGINNING AGAIN

Ezra 1:1–11

After Christmas festivities conclude at the end of December, my thoughts often turn to the coming year. While my children are out of school and our daily rhythms are slow, I reflect on where the last year has brought me and where I hope the next will take me. Those reflections sometimes come with pain and regret over the mistakes I've made. Yet the prospect of starting a new year fills me with hope and expectancy. I feel I have the opportunity to begin again with a fresh start, no matter what the last year held.

My anticipation of a fresh start pales in comparison to the sense of hope the Israelites must have felt when Cyrus, the king of Persia, released them to return to their homeland in Judah after seventy long years of captivity in Babylon. The previous king, Nebuchadnezzar, had deported the Israelites from their homeland. But the Lord prompted Cyrus to send the captives home to Jerusalem to rebuild God's temple (Ezra 1:2–3). Cyrus also returned to them many of the treasures that had been taken from the temple. Their lives as God's chosen people in the land God had appointed to them began afresh after a long season of hardship in Babylon as a consequence for their sin.

No matter what lies in our past, when we confess our sin, God forgives us and gives us a fresh start. What great cause for hope!

—*Kirsten*

Relive the joy of sins forgiven by confessing known transgressions to your Savior

The Writers

Alyson Kieda has been an editor for Our Daily Bread Ministries for over a decade and has more than thirty-five years of editing experience. Alyson has loved writing since she was a child and is thrilled to be writing for *Our Daily Bread*. She is married with three adult children and a growing number of grandchildren. Alyson loves reading, walking in the woods, and being with family. She feels blessed to be following in her mother's footsteps—she wrote articles many years ago for another devotional.

Amy Boucher Pye is a writer, editor, and speaker. The author of *Finding Myself in Britain: Our Search for Faith, Home, and True Identity* and a devotional book *The Living Cross* lives in London. She runs the Woman Alive book club in the United Kingdom and enjoys life with her family in their English vicarage.

Anne Cetas became a follower of Jesus in her late teens. At nineteen, she was given a copy of *Our Daily Bread* by a friend. She also devoured Discovery Series topical study booklets from Our Daily Bread Ministries. Several years later, she joined the editorial staff of *Our Daily Bread* as a proofreader. Anne began writing for the devotional booklet in September 2004 and moved all the way up to being executive editor for the publication. Anne is now retired; she and her husband, Carl, enjoy walking and bicycling together. They volunteer as mentors in an urban ministry.

Bree Rostic is a writer, speaker, spoken word artist, and communication specialist with Our Daily Bread Ministries. Bree's passion is sharing God's love for women to see healing and restoration. She gained her admiration for the Word of God through serving as a teacher in her local ministry. Breonna is married to Daryle, and together they raise their three kids in Grand Rapids, Michigan.

Cindy Hess Kasper served for more than forty years at Our Daily Bread Ministries. She learned a love for singing and working with words from her father, Clair Hess, longtime senior editor for the ministry. Now retired, Cindy and her husband, Tom, have three grown children and seven grandchildren, in whom they take great delight.

Elisa Morgan, perhaps best known for her long tenure as CEO of MOPS International, lives in Colorado with her husband, Evan. She now cohosts two programs with Our Daily Bread Ministries— *Discover the Word* for radio and the *God Hears Her* podcast—and continues to write books on the Christian life, spiritual formation, and evangelism, including *When We Pray Like Jesus* and *You Are Not Alone*.

Jennifer Benson Schuldt has been writing professionally since 1997 when she graduated from Cedarville University and began her career as a technical writer. Jennifer lives in the Chicago suburbs with her husband, Bob, and their two children. When she isn't writing or serving at home and church, she enjoys painting and reading poetry and fiction.

Joanie Yoder and her husband established a Christian rehabilitation center for drug addicts in England many years ago. After being widowed, she wrote a book, *Finding the God-Dependent Life*, which was published by this ministry. Joanie went home to heaven in 2004.

Julie Ackerman Link, after a lengthy battle with cancer, went to be with the Lord on April 10, 2015. Julie began writing articles each month for *Our Daily Bread* in 2000. She was a popular author with *Our Daily Bread* readers, and her insightful and inspiring articles have touched millions of lives around the world. Julie also wrote the books *Above All, Love* and *A Heart for God*, published by Our Daily Bread Publishing (ODBP). Her book *100 Prayers Inspired by the Psalms* was published posthumously by ODBP in 2017.

Keila Ochoa and her husband have two young children. She helps Media Associates International with their training ministry for writers around the world and has written several books in Spanish for children, teens, and women. She serves in her church in the areas of youth, missions, and women's ministry.

Kirsten Holmberg is a speaker, author, and coach based in the Pacific Northwest. She's the author of *Advent with the Word: Approaching Christmas Through the Inspired Language of God* and several Bible studies. She speaks regularly at business, church, and community events, encouraging others to step closer to Jesus and better know His love for them through His Word. Find her online at kirstenholmberg.com or on Facebook, Twitter, and Instagram (@kirholmberg).

Lisa Samra desires to see Christ glorified in her life and in the ministries she serves. Born and raised in Texas, Lisa is always on the lookout for sweet tea and brisket. She graduated with a BA in journalism from the University of Texas and earned a Master of Biblical Studies degree from Dallas Theological Seminary. Lisa now lives in Grand Rapids, Michigan, with her husband, Jim, and their four children. Jim is pastor of the church started by the founder of Our Daily Bread Ministries, Dr. M. R. DeHaan.

Lori Hatcher and her husband live delightfully close to their four grandchildren in Lexington, South Carolina. The author of three devotional books and a blog, she loves to mine God's Word for treasure and share what she uncovers. She is the author of the Our Daily Bread Publishing book *Refresh Your Faith*.

Marion Stroud went to be with her Savior on August 8, 2015, after a battle with cancer. Two of her popular books of prayers, *Dear God, It's Me and It's Urgent* and *It's Just You and Me, Lord*, were published by Our Daily Bread Publishing. Marion worked as a cross-cultural trainer for Media Associates International, helping writers produce books for their own culture.

Patricia Raybon, a former *Sunday Magazine* editor at *The Denver Post* and former associate professor of journalism at the University of Colorado at Boulder, now writes bridge-building books "to inspire people to love God and each other." Passionate for God's Word, she also supports Bible-translation projects worldwide. Her award-winning books include *My First White Friend* and *I Told the Mountain to Move*. A mother of two and grandmother of five, she and husband Dan live in Colorado. Find her at patriciaraybon. com or on Facebook or Twitter @patriciaraybon.

Poh Fang Chia never dreamed of being in a language-related profession; chemistry was her first love. The turning point came when she received Jesus as her Savior as a fifteen-year-old and expressed to Jesus that she would like to create books that touch lives. She serves with Our Daily Bread Ministries at the Singapore office as an editor and is also a member of the Chinese editorial review committee.

Remi Oyedele is freelance writer with twin passions for God's Word and children's books. Her ultimate life goal is to shape scriptural truths into stories for children and children at heart. Remi has an MA in writing for children. A native of Nigeria, she currently resides in Central Florida where she spends her spare time reading and blogging at wordzpread.com. Remi is married to David, her number one blog fan.

Xochitl (soh-cheel) Dixon equips and encourages readers to embrace God's grace and grow deeper in their personal relationships with Christ and others. Serving as an author, speaker, and blogger at xedixon.com, she enjoys singing, reading, photography, motherhood, and being married to her best friend Dr. W. Alan Dixon Sr., a college professor. You can find out about her books at ourdailybreadpublishing.org.